CRAZYSHOT!
Companion

Charted Designs for Overshot Weaving on the Rigid Heddle Loom

Myra Wood

A Woodworks Editions book
www.myrawood.com

First printing: November 2021
ISBN: 978-0-9800182-6-4, 0-9800182-6-9

Editing by Sarah Peasley
Book and cover design, illustration and charts, photography: Myra Wood
e-mail: myra@woodworksart.com
www.myrawood.com

Contents

I love gridded charts. All kinds of gridded needlework charts. I read them like sheet music and recite the stitch patterns in my head while I work across each row to my own rhythm.

Charts are the backbone of many fiber arts - a fact I find endlessly satisfying. The beauty of the simple, gridded charts contained within is that they can be applied to any form of needlecraft, including weaving, stranded color knitting, Kogin embroidery, and counted cross-stitch.

Since this book is written as a companion to Crazyshot: Creative Overshot Weaving on the Rigid Heddle Loom, I've included samples of each chart woven with the single heddle overshot technique.

In Crazyshot, you'll find all the information you need on that creative weaving technique.

The purpose of this companion book is to give you a generous sampling of building blocks to play with. Included within are also all the tools you need to use, create, and modify charts for anything you'd like. If you'd like more information on the basic technique, you can find it in the first Crazyshot book.

There are a bazillion ways to repeat and/or combine charted patterns to create an infinite number of unique fabrics and borders. The charts presented here can be used alone or together since they are all based on common multiples of 5. You can mix and match them to your heart's content.

The combinations are endless and I hope the possibilities excite and inspire your creativity as much as they do mine.

Reading the Charts

Charts are read starting in the lower right corner of the grid. Read the first row across from right to left, then move up to the second row and read from right to left again. Continue, traveling up one row at a time, from bottom to top. If you are left-handed, you can reverse these directions and read from left to right if it's more comfortable to do so. The charts only show the pattern rows and it's assumed that the plain or tabby fabric is woven alternating the heddle position every other row.

The dark chart squares indicate the pattern: a worked stitch or covered warp. The light squares indicate the back-ground: an unworked stitch, a stitch of another color, or an exposed warp.

Very simply put, each charted pattern row is followed by inserting the pickup stick across the warp in neutral position, under white squares to raise the warp and over dark squares to cover the warp. The pattern yarn is drawn across the shed, over and under the warp following the patterns according to the chart.

Note that although the chart grids are square, the designs, when woven, will appear to be squashed a bit vertically.

To compensate for this, use a thicker tabby weft or pattern yarn, or you can repeat each pattern row twice if the pattern yarn is closer in size to the tabby yarn.

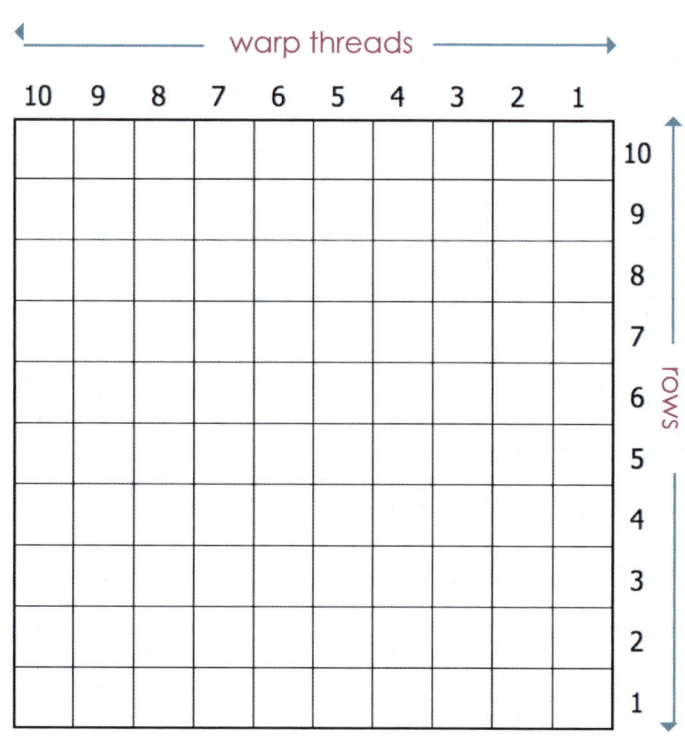

Selvedges

Selvedges are never included in the charts. When determining the total number of warp threads needed for weaving, calculate the total warp threads needed for the width of the fabric, then add two additional warp threads for the selvedges: one for each selvedge on either side of the charted areas.

As you work across each row, wrap the yarn around the beginning selvedge thread, follow the chart row to the last warp thread, then wrap the yarn around that ending selvedge thread.

The pick-up stick will be inserted in the same direction as each chart row is read, from right to left or from left to right depending on your dominant hand preference.

The charts only show the pattern rows. A pick-up stick is used to create the pattern by going over or under each warp thread according to the chart: over dark squares to cover the warp, and under light squares to show the warp.

Dark squares in a chart denote the pattern; light squares are the background. You may instead be using a light color for the pattern and a dark color for the background, but reading the chart and placing the pick-up stick will always be the same: dark squares over, light squares under. There was a suggestion on one of the online forums to think of the dark and light squares as "Dover" and "Lunder" to keep track of the path of the pick-up stick.

The color of the squares has nothing to do with the color of the yarn. You may be using a dark warp and a light pattern yarn. Although it's counter-intuitive, make sure your pick-up stick is inserted following the chart. Remember that dark squares mean the pick-up stick is placed OVER the warp thread and light squares mean the pick-up stick is placed UNDER the warp thread.

The charts in the book are color-coded to match the weaving samples. Feel free to use any colors you'd like.

 Pick-up stick **OVER** warp threads

 Pick-up stick **UNDER** warp threads

Floats

For overshot weaving, it is assumed that a plain background (tabby) fabric is woven simultaneously every other row. To show off the pattern at its best, this fabric is best woven as a more weft-faced weave, rather than as a balanced weave.

The pattern yarn traveling over and under the warp is called the supplementary weft or the "floats." Even if the pattern yarn only goes over or under one warp thread, that's still considered a float since it's part of the charted pattern, not part of the background fabric.

The lengths of the floats influence the overall design. Short floats over one warp thread tend to look like small spots, or like a thin line when repeated over multiple rows, whereas wider floats of 3 to 5 covered warp threads create a thicker line.

The more warp threads that are covered, the thicker the motif will appear on the front surface of the fabric. Due to the reversible nature of overshot weaving, the motifs will also appear as a "negative" image of the chart on the back of the fabric.

I prefer variation in the number of warps crossed, in order to create a more complicated yet balanced look. Most of the patterns included in the charts within this book are combinations of 1, 3, and 5 warp floats, but some incorporate 2, 4, and 6 warp floats as well.

A good rule of thumb is to keep the floats crossing over or under 1 to 5 warp threads at a time. A few floats can travel over 6 or 7 warps, but it is generally considered best for the integrity and durability of the fabric to cover no more than 7 if you intend to use both the front and the back of the fabric. In some cases, with a finer yarn and a closer sett, you may be able to incorporate longer floats without compromising the integrity of the fabric. If you will never see or use the reverse side, then you can make an exception, since the longer floats on the back won't be exposed or catch on anything.

One of my favorite things about Crazyshot fabric is it's reversible, giving you even more pattern options.

pattern (right side)　　　　　　　　　　　　　　*reverse pattern (opposite side)*

Horizontal multiples

One complete chart row for each pattern is called a multiple, and multiples can be repeated horizontally as many times as desired. The easiest way to achieve this is to use a total number of warp threads that is evenly divisible by the number of warp threads in one multiple.

For a completely symmetrical chart pattern, mirror the leftmost column of the chart by adding an identical column at the left side, and add one more warp to the total count (you will now be warping an odd number of ends, which means your last slot will only contain one end, not two). Unless you are featuring the pattern as a centered focal point, perfect symmetry may not really be necessary.

At times you may need to use a total number of warp threads that is not evenly divisible by the multiple. To keep the pattern centered, first determine the number of full multiples that can be worked within the total number of warp threads needed. Divide the remaining warp threads by 2, then count that many squares in from the rightmost column of the chart. Begin weaving a partial pattern multiple with that column, then continue across the warp with full multiples, ending with a matching partial pattern multiple.

Another method to use when partial multiples are required is to find both the center of the design on the chart and the center warp thread, then count the number of warp threads to the right of center to determine where on the chart to start weaving.

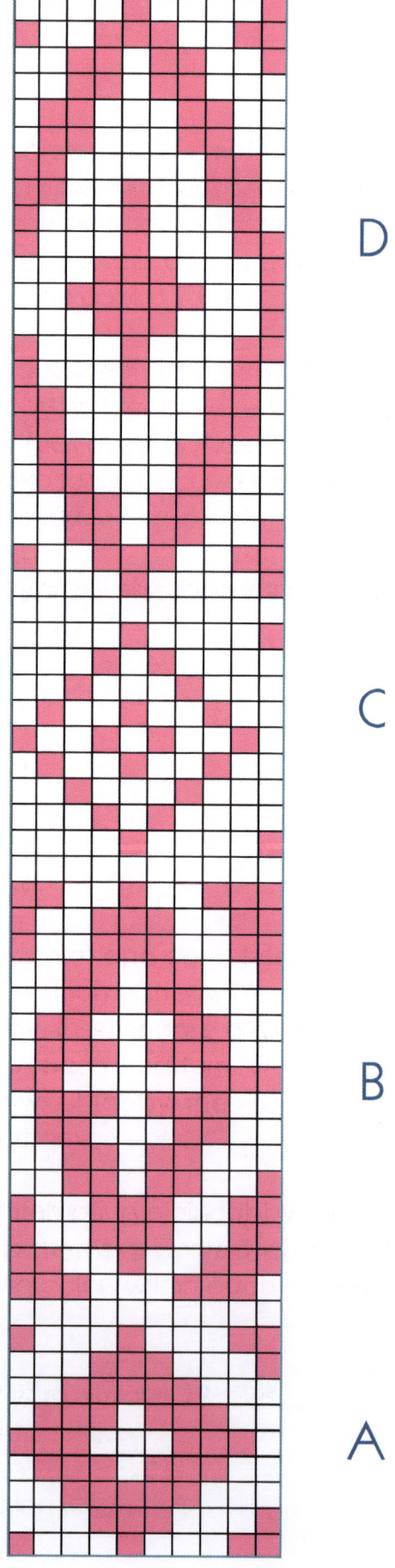

D

C

B

A

D
C
B
A

Patterns can be stacked vertically, either separated by spaces of plain background (tabby), or placed consecutively as long as the patterns merge well and are pleasing to the eye.

Multiple repeats of the same charted pattern can create an overall design on the fabric both horizontally and vertically.

For reasons of symmetry, I duplicated the first and last rows of the included charts as if they were only going to be woven once, and as a result the patterns are mirrored at the bottom and top. If you want to repeat one of these charts vertically, delete the last chart row and repeat the pattern from bottom to top as many times as you'd like.

horizontal and vertical repeats of E

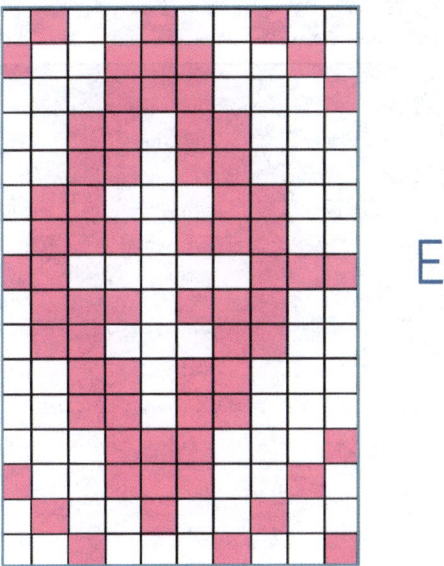

E

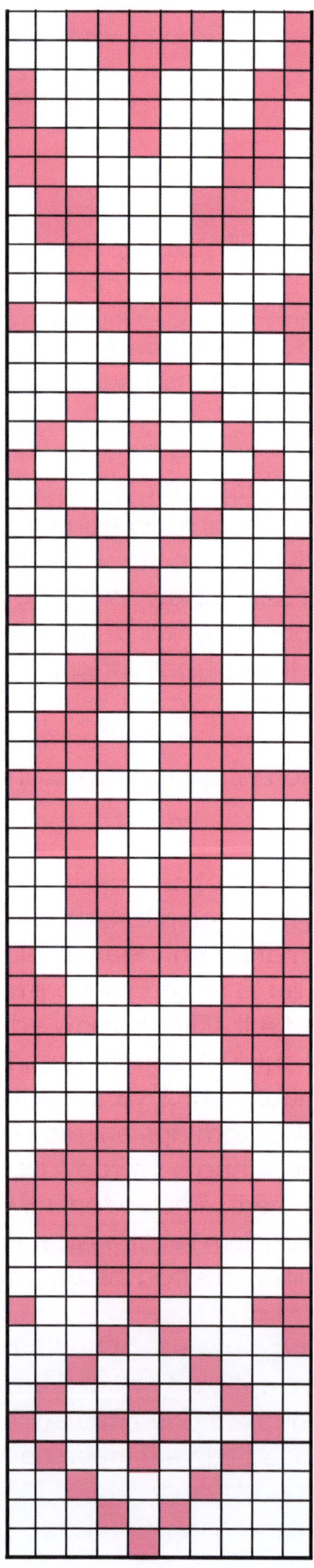

When stacking different charted patterns vertically, it may be necessary to delete or add rows between them so the fabric flows nicely from one design into the other.

Color is a very personal matter. My best advice is to pick colors you love and make sure you're happy with them before you start weaving.

The more contrast there is between the colors, the better the pattern will show up. Most patterns look more intense if they're light on a dark background, but you can get stunning combinations with any color as the base. If you are looking for a subtle pattern, pick colors that are close together in value. If you prefer a monochromatic textured fabric like a brocade, use different yarns of the same color.

There is a series of books I recommend called The Designer's Guide to Color 1-4 by Ikuyoshu Shibukawa and Yumi Takahashi, which gives you palette after palette of endless color combinations. Another good way to choose color combinations is to look at a printed fabric you love and match yarn colors to it. Or look at a variegated yarn as a source for choosing solid colors.

I like to use solid or semi-solid colors for the background and pattern yarns so that the design doesn't get obscured by the fluctuations in color. Variegated yarns, especially when used for the pattern yarn, will usually obscure the design. You may be able to get away with a variegated tabby yarn if all of its colors are about the same value, but if there is too much contrast between the colors, it won't work.

There really are no rules, so my best suggestion is to swatch first and see what you prefer.

Any of the charted patterns can be broken up into several colors. I generally pick 2-4 colors.

If you have a drawing program, you can select colors based on the yarns you have chosen, then select specific squares and change the colors to see how they work together.

recycled salad boxes make great yarn storage containers

I find it much easier to concentrate on the pick-up pattern when the colors on the chart match my yarn colors.

There's a wonderful, free chart-making program available online at:
www.stitchfiddle.com/en

You may want to take some time and re-color a chosen chart to match your yarn choice.

charts 99, 105 and 110
chart colorized to match the yarn

warp: Valley Yarns Valley Cotton 3/2, Black
tabby weft: Valley Yarns Charlemont, Black
pattern weft: Universal Yarn, Deluxe Worsted,
Turquoise, Orchid, Lime Tree, Hot Fuscia, Cactus,
Blue Lagoon

I highly recommend swatching a small sample before starting any large project to see if you like the the choice of yarns and to try alternatives to see what you like best to show off the pattern. And measuring gauge is crucial if you want the final fabric to be a specific size. You can use a smaller loom for swatching as long as the heddle size is the same.

Start by warping 42 ends (40 + 2 for selvedges). Weave an inch vertically of just the background yarn, then pick a simple diamond pattern like the ones on page 23 and complete one or two entire repeats. This is also a good time to try different gauges for wefts per inch-different sections can be woven with a firmer or softer beat to try out different drapes of the fabric.

Weave a few more rows of just background yarn and then several rows of waste yarn. There's no need for a hemstitch, since this sample is just for measuring gauge.

Measure how many warp threads and weft rows equal 1"/25mm both horizontally and vertically, then remove the fabric from the loom. Wet finish the sample the same way you will treat the final piece, and then measure the warp and weft gauges again.

Multiply the number of warp threads per 1"/10mm of finished fabric by the desired fabric width. Add two warp threads for the selvedges, and then you're ready to warp your loom.

Multiply the number of weft rows per 1"/25mm of finished fabric by the desired fabric length. Weaving to that total number of rows will give you the length you want based on the gauge of your sample.

example: 21 tabby wefts per inch

Translating weaving drafts

Overshot drafts are drawn for multi-shaft looms, but can be translated and used for single-heddle overshot.

There's an entire library of free pattern drafts available in the public domain at handweaving.net, made possible by Ralph Griswold. If you use this resource, please consider thanking and helping Mr. Griswold by making a donation here: https://handweaving.net/ways-to-help.

Particularly of interest are drafts from Pattern Book Drafts by Heinrich Böscher (1819), and Point Threaded Drafts for 8 Shafts by Rebecca Logan (2021). The example on the next page is from the second book. See: handweaving.net #79316.

Download and save any of the large files you want to use from this website. Whether you are redrawing by hand or using a digital paint program, you'll need to resize the pattern draft to 8.5" x 11". Print out a copy of the full draft and then, using a pencil and a ruler, locate and isolate one repeat of the pattern as follows:

After choosing a motif and printing out the pattern draft, identify the column that you consider to be the start of the motif and draw a vertical line to the right of this column, from the top of the chart to the bottom.

Follow the motif horizontally across the draft from right to left until you reach a column that is identical to the one you started with. Draw a second vertical line to the right of this column. The two lines designate one full horizontal repeat of the motif, and determine the number of warps needed per repeat.

Now identify the row that you consider to be the bottom of the motif, and draw a horizontal line across the chart beneath this row. Follow the motif up vertically until you reach a row that is identical to the one you started with. Draw a second horizontal line beneath this row. The two lines designate one full vertical repeat of the motif.

The isolated area now indicates the number of warp threads and the rows of pattern weft needed to complete a full motif. Enlarge the pattern repeat and print it out or enlarge it to fit 8.5" x 11".

Extend all of the lines across the image horizontally and vertically.

At this point you can re-draw and fill in the chart grid, either by hand or on the computer.

*sample shows
draft # 79316
handweaving.net*

8 Shafts, 8 Treadles	Single Pattern Unit	Repeats Shown		Maximum Floats	Front	Back
Threading	14	6		Warp	5	5
Treadling	14	4		Weft	5	5

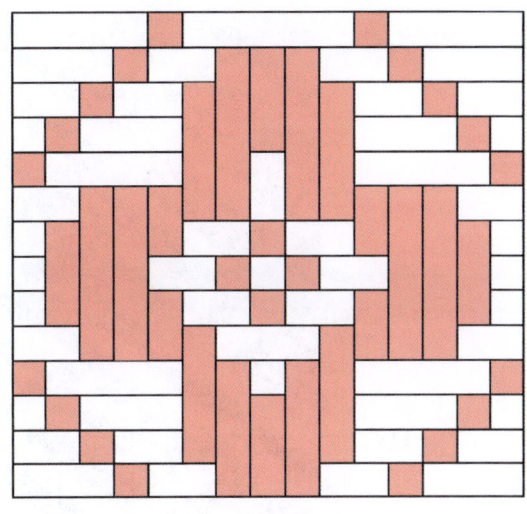

one repeat from original draft

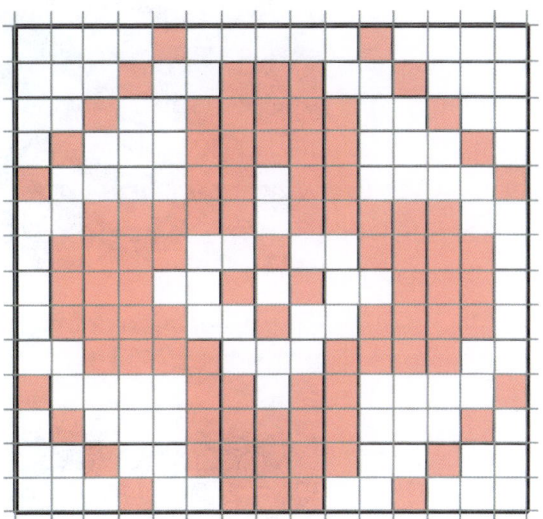

all lines extended on print-out.

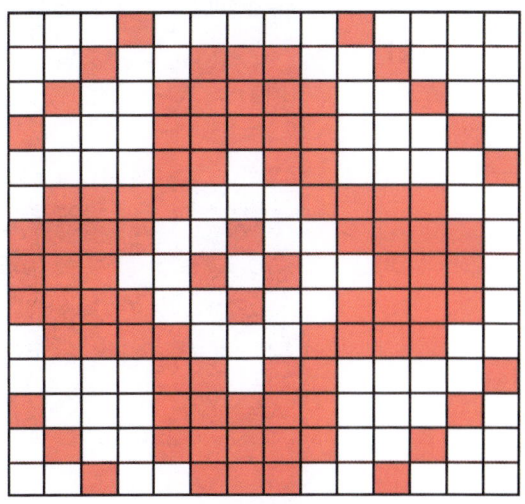

redrawn in graphics program

Drawing your own designs

There are many, many resources for charted designs. My absolute favorite is Alice Starmore's Charts for Color Knitting (2011), which includes tons of useable motifs. Absolutely any charted design can be modified for overshot weaving.

You may come across a design you want to use that is not charted, or you may want to design and draw your own patterns. This is easily done with some graph paper and a pencil, or with a computer drawing program. I use digital graph paper and my computer. I search for "graph paper" on Google, then I open that file in Photoshop, where I can select and fill in the desired squares.

Draw the entire design symmetrically, following the chosen motif as closely as possible. Make sure to mirror the design from left to right and from top to bottom. One easy way to do this is to draw one quarter of the design digitally and then cut and paste, rotating that initial quadrant three times to fill in the complete motif. In this manner you'll achieve a perfectly symmetrical design.

If you can take a picture of the design, or if you have a simple chart you just want to redraw, you can load the picture or chart into a photo editor and try to align it as closely as possible to the program's grid. Sometimes this works, and sometimes it proves to be more

trouble than it's worth.

I like a nice mix of small and large floats to create interest in the design. You may find a wonderful charted design you'd like to use that has longer-than-desirable floats. You can always modify a chart to break up a long float by inserting one light square in the middle of the dark squares making up the long float or vice-versa. Small plus signs also work well to fill in wider spaces.

original chart

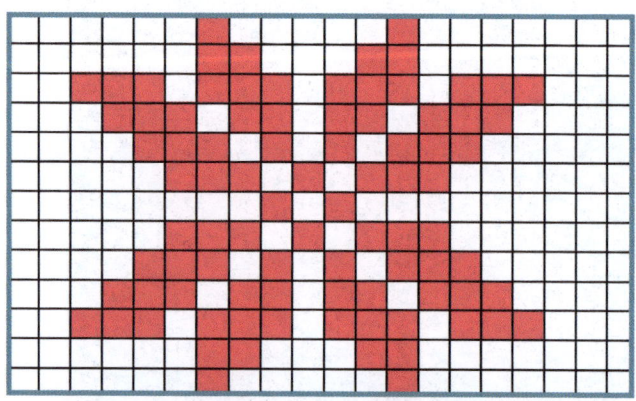

redrawn with addition of inserted floats

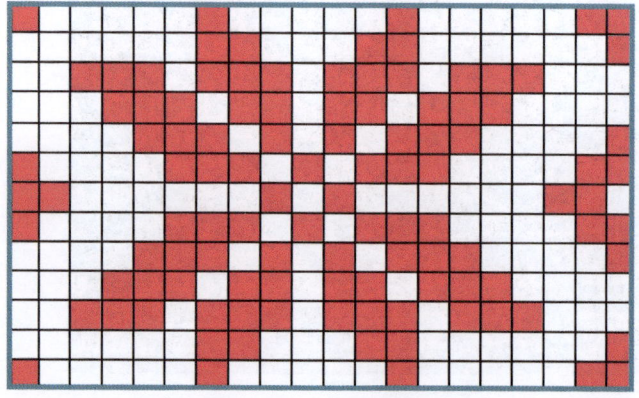

The pattern isn't showing up well.

• The pattern yarn may be too thin in comparison to the background (tabby) yarn. Try a thicker pattern yarn.

• The pattern yarn may not have enough contrast with the background (tabby) color. Try a pattern yarn with more color contrast.

The pattern appears too squashed vertically.

• Try a thicker pattern yarn.

• Work each row of the pattern twice.

• Hold two strands of your pattern yarn together.

The sides are pulling in.

• On the edges, leave a little more slack with the pattern yarn than you normally would. Overshot has a tendency to draw in, so you don't need to pull too tightly.

• Some patterns include long floats at the beginning and end of a row - make sure the weft is wrapped around the selvedge warp threads.

• Make sure to wrap the selvedge warp threads with both the pattern and the tabby weft yarns.

A pattern row is incorrect.

• It's important to check each pattern row to make sure your weaving matches the chart. It's good to get into the habit of checking each row to the chart after passing the pattern yarn through the shed, before removing the pick-up stick.

• Sometimes you may miss an error and continue for a few rows. In this case, you need to unweave back to the incorrect row and reset the pick-up stick according to the pattern for that row.

• The tabby is easily unwoven by placing the heddle in the appropriate shed and taking the shuttle back through the shed.

• The pattern yarn needs to be unpicked by placing the same path the yarn is following. It's easiest to do this by bringing the pattern yarn up to a 45 degree angle.

Stitches appear to be missing.

• Sometimes single warp floats don't show up well or may be obscured by the weft rows above or below. You can vertically needle weave a single strand of warp yarn right over the weft pattern here, or anywhere you want to emphasis a vertical line.

How to use this book

All of the charts in this book are multiples of 5, 10, 20 or 30. Patterns with the same multiple are centered over each other so that they will flow from any one into another seamlessly.

In some cases the last row of the chart may duplicate the first. Check and see if that's the case and delete either the first or last row so it doesn't repeat and begin the multiple again from bottom to top.

Each chart is numbered with a corresponding photo of it woven in one full repeating horizontal pattern across the warp. I've also included sample photos of some of the multiples repeated vertically as an all-over pattern. Any of the patterns can be repeated vertically and horizontally to fit the size of the fabric you want to weave. Try and keep the number of warps divisible by 10, 20 or 30, depending on the charts you choose.

All of the samples are woven with a size 3 cotton warp, a sport-weight wool tabby weft and a worsted-weight wool pattern weft.

I've include a scarf and mug rug pattern in this book that can be used as the basis for your own designs. Using the same type of equipment, yarn weights, sett and weaving directions, you can substitute any of these patterns as you'd like.

You can be as free-style or structured as you'd like. Copy the repeats you want to include onto a piece of graph paper (or make a copy of the ones provided at the end of the book) and see how they flow together. This is a good time to make any alterations to the pattern if you'd like.

Or you can just pick any one of the designs randomly and leave a few rows of tabby between the patterns.

This book can be used with any of the projects in Crazyshot: Creative Overshot Weaving for the Rigid Heddle Loom. Follow the same directions for any of the projects and substitute any patterns as you'd like.

If you'd like to make a wider or narrower fabric, make sure to add or subtract in multiples of 10 or 20 depending on your designs and also remember to add 2 extra warps for the selvedges.

Resources:
- myrawood.com - my website
- kromskina.com - Kromski Presto loom
- stitchfiddle.com/en - charting program
- stitches.events - virtual fiber art classes
- kelly-casanova-weaving-lessons. teachable.com- Kelly Casanova's online weaving school

repeats of chart 28

repeats of chart 33

repeats of chart 33 - opposite side

34

35

36

37

38

39

40

41

42

43

44
45
46
47
48
49
50
51
52
53
54
55
56
57
58
59
60
61
62
63

44

45

46

47

48

49

50

51

52

53

repeats of chart 51

repeats of chart 52

54

55

56

57

58

59

60

61

62

63

repeats of chart 66

64
65
66

67
68
69

70
71
72

73
74

64

65

66

67

68

69

70

71

72

73

74

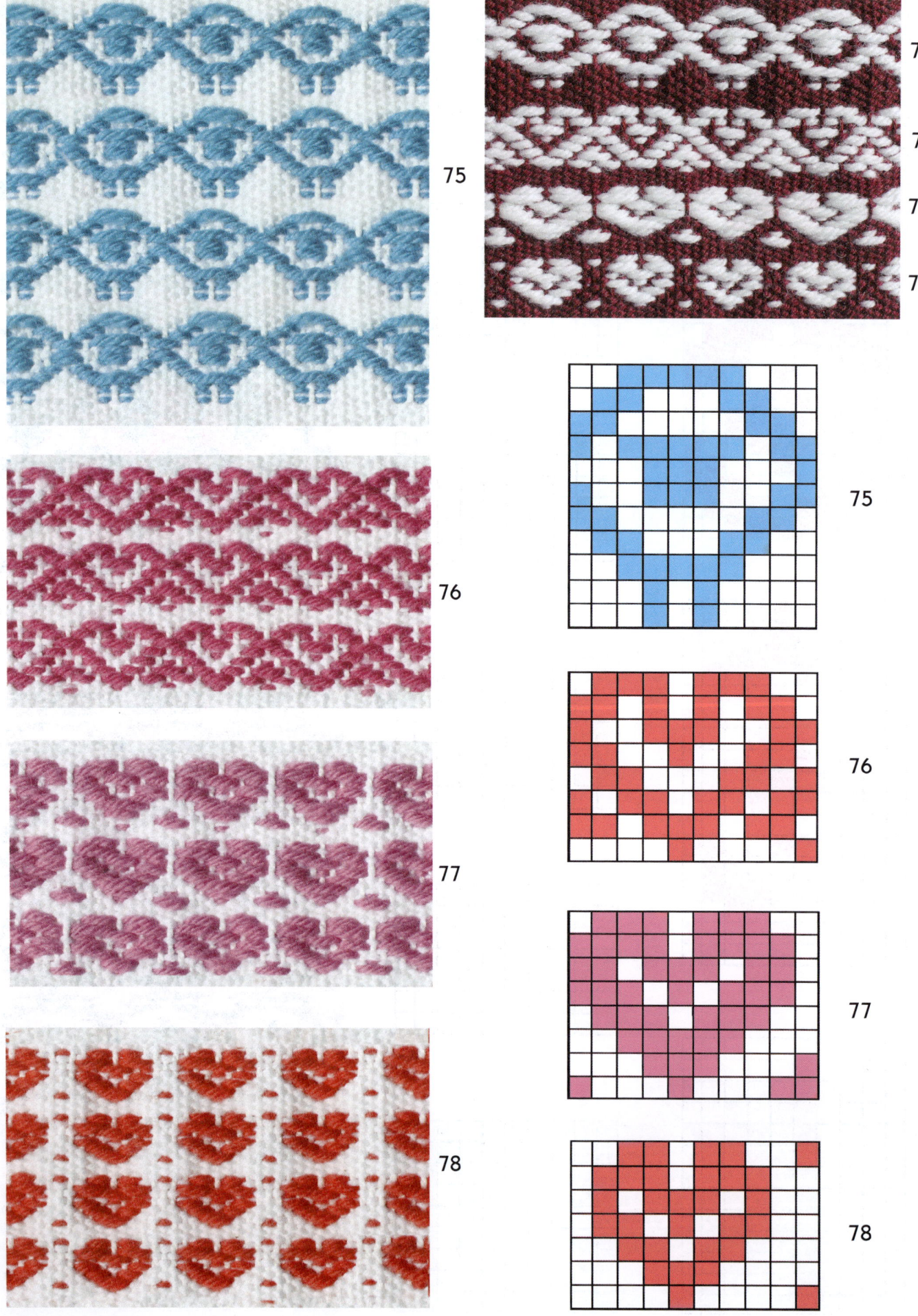

75

76

77

78

75

76

77

78

28

79

80

81

82

83

84

85

86

87

88

89

90

91

79

80

81

82

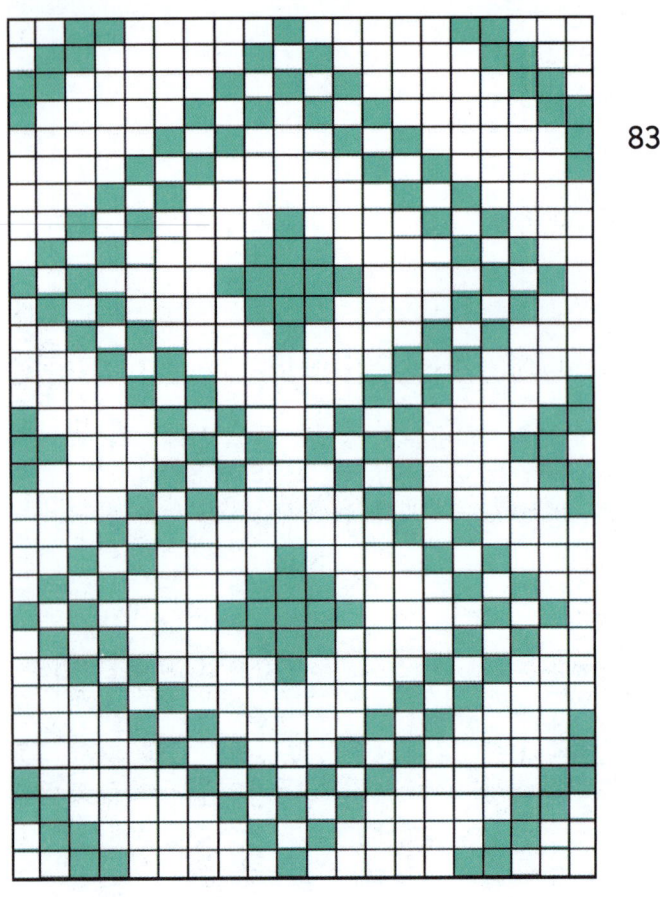

83

repeats of chart 82 - right side

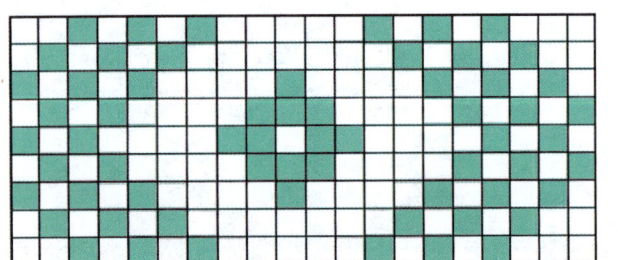

84

repeats of chart 82 - opposite side

85

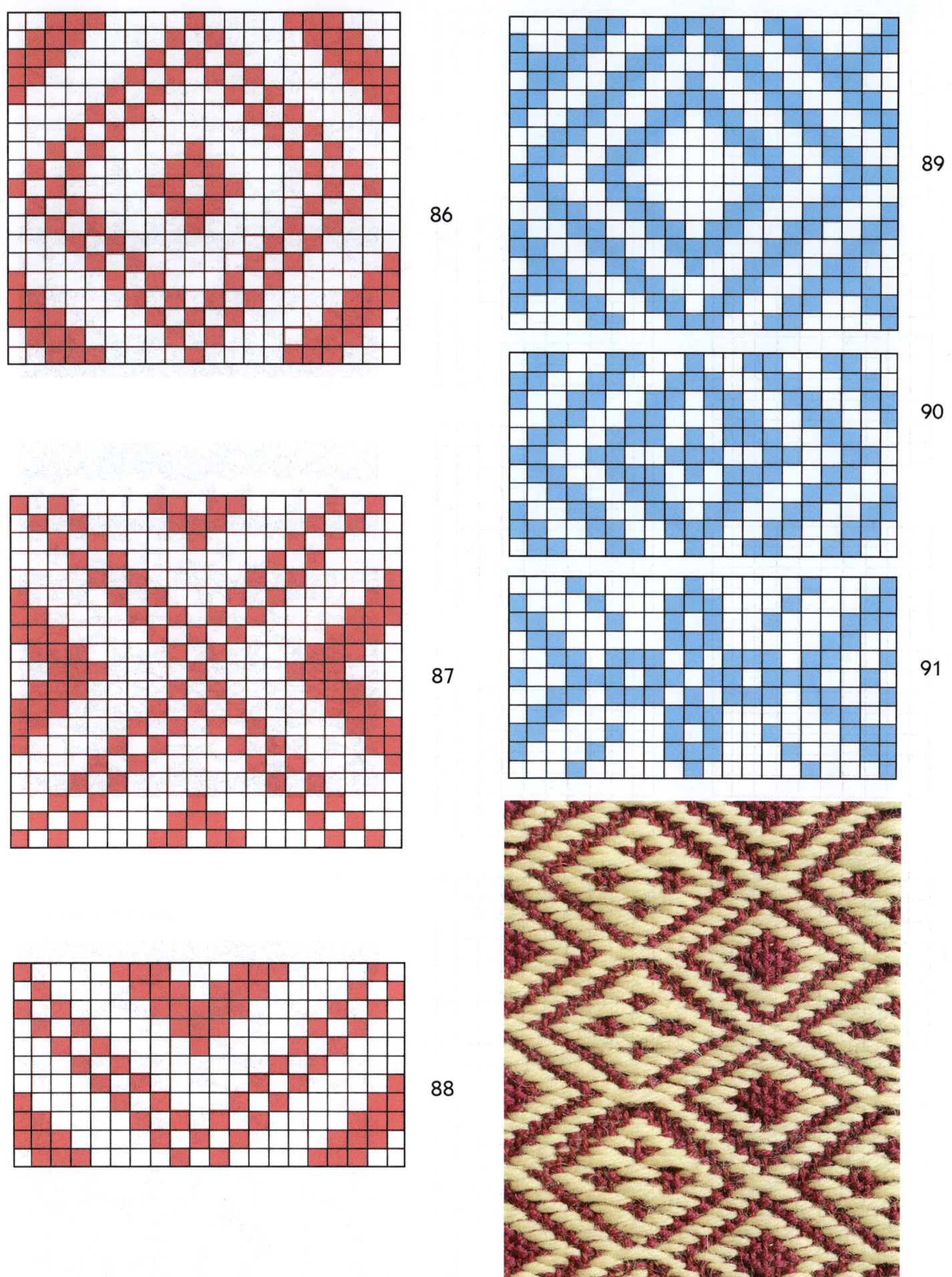

86

89

87

90

91

88

repeats of chart 89

92

93

94

95

96

97

98

99

100

101

102

103

104

105

92

93

94

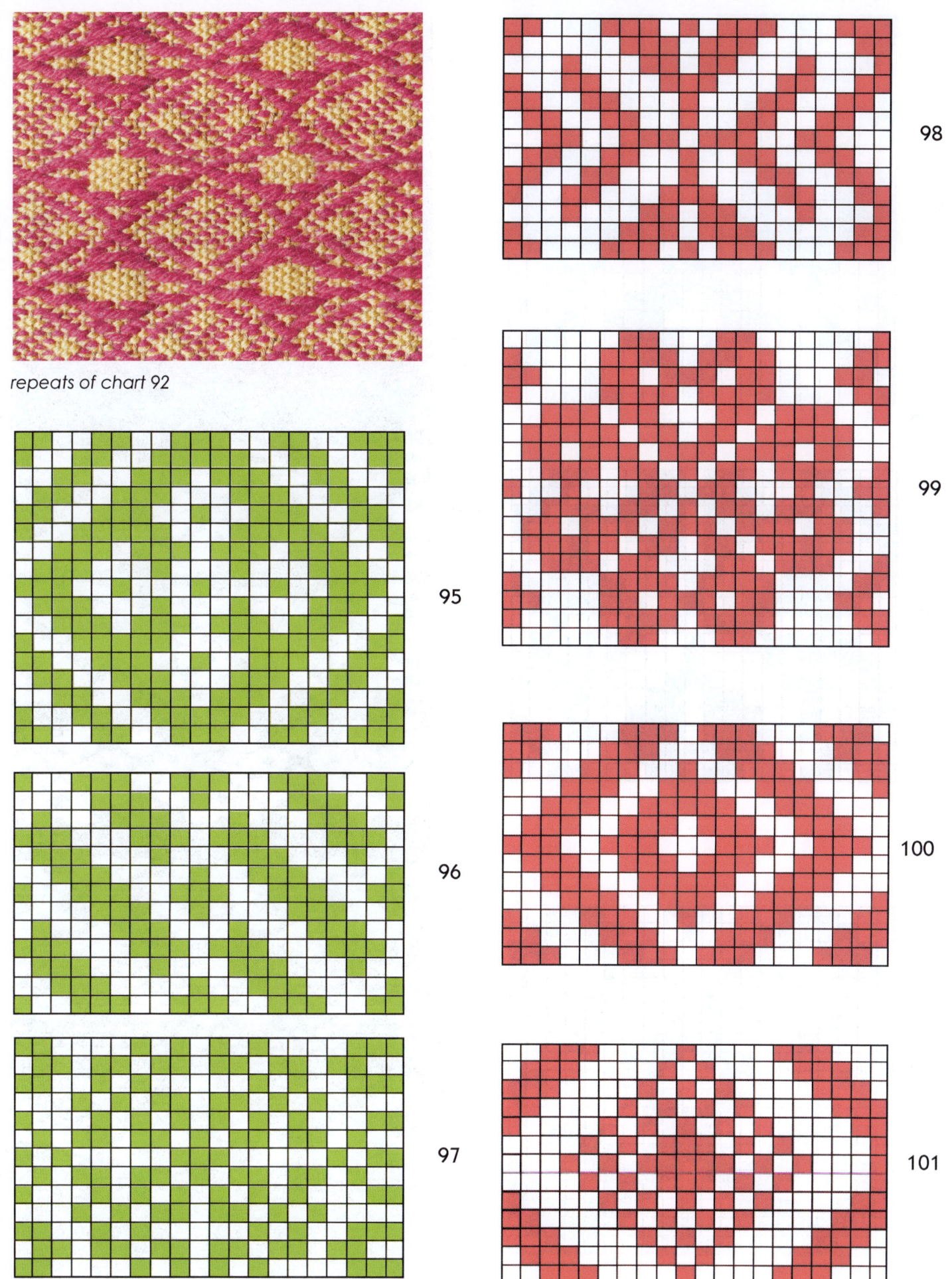

repeats of chart 92

95

96

97

98

99

100

101

33

102

103

repeats of 104 - right side

repeats of chart 104 - opposite side

104

105

106

107

108

109

110

111

112

113

114

106

107

108

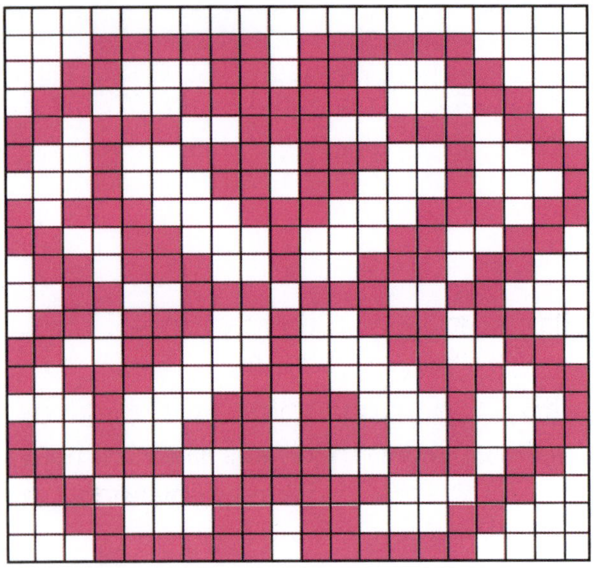

109

110

111

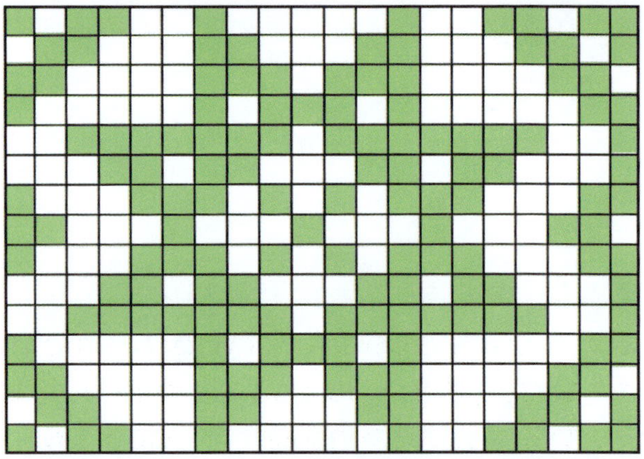

112

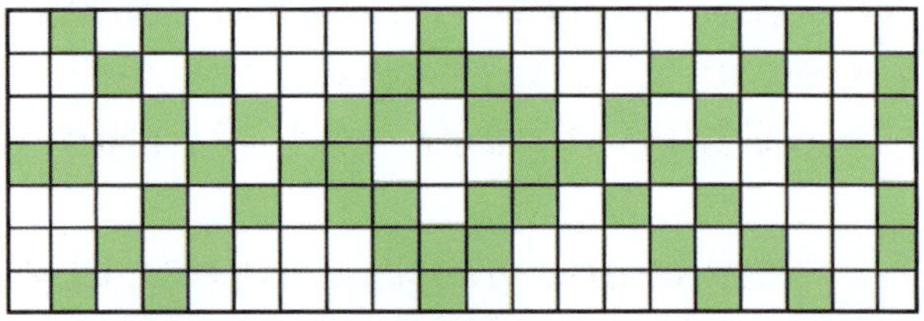

113

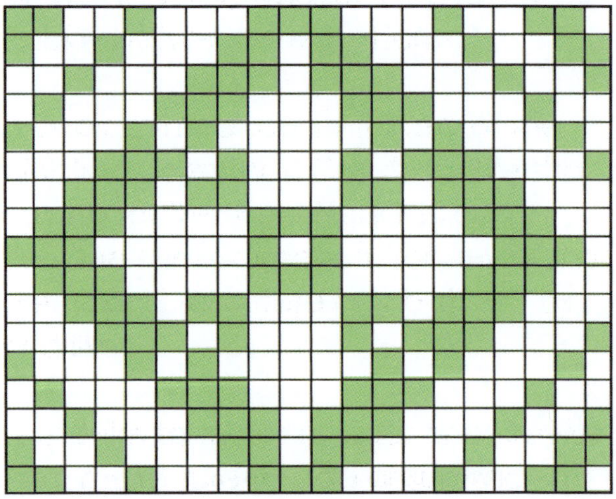

114

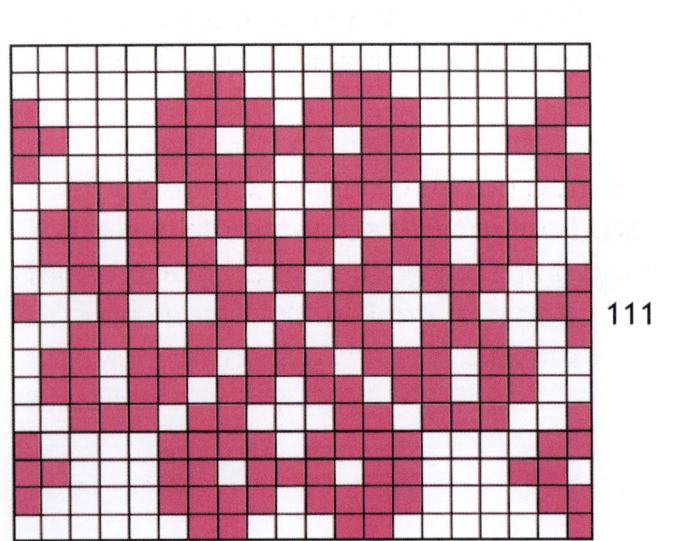

repeats of chart 111

36

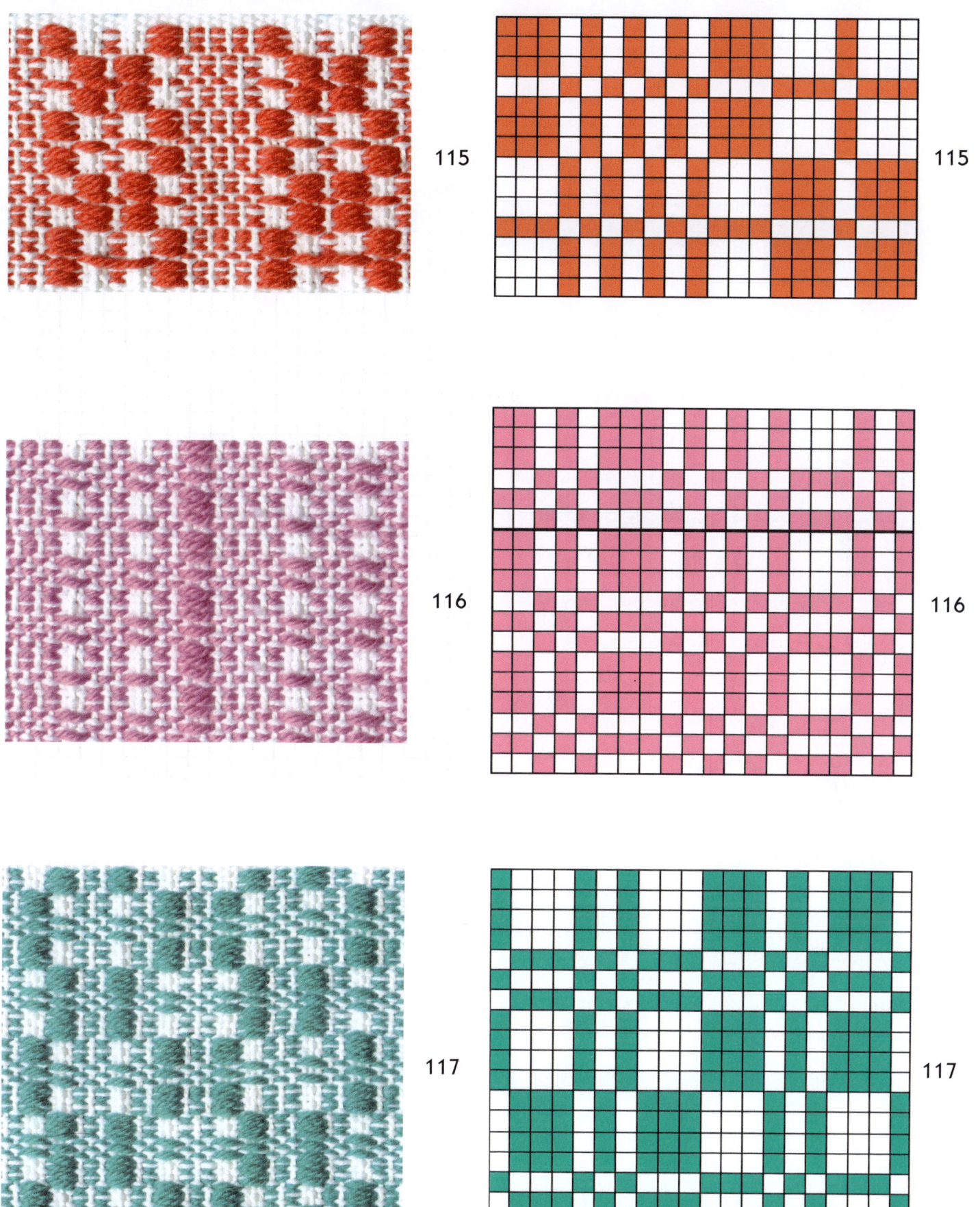

115

115

116

116

117

117

118

repeats of chart 118 - opposite side

repeats of chart 118 - right side

119

repeats of chart 119 - opposite side

repeats of chart 119

120

121

120

121

122

123

122

123

124

125

124

125

Equipment

10" rigid heddle loom or larger with a 7.5 or 8 dent heddle, 2 shuttles, pick-up stick, tapestry needle

Yarn

Warp:
3/2 or 8/4 cotton or cotton-rayon blend or size 3 crochet cotton yarn, 175 yds (Lion Brand Comfy Cotton Blend Yarn, Ocean Breeze)

Weft (tabby):
Sport-weight wool or wool/silk blend, 300 yds (Malabrigo Rios, Teal Feather, Zarzamorra)

Weft (pattern yarn):
Worsted-weight wool or wool/silk blend, 50 yds or more of 3-5 colors (Malabrigo Silky Merino, Purple Mystery, Azules, Indiecita)

Sett

Warp: 7.5 epi

7.5 epi x 22 ppi = 1" tabby woven on loom

Total warp ends: 62
(60 + 2 for selvedges)

Dimensions

Width on the loom: 7"

Warp length:
94" (68" + 6" for fringe, and 20" for loom waste)

Finished size: 6.5" x 68", without fringe

Magical Mystery Scarf

More of a recipe than a specific pattern, this silky scarf calls for a wool or acrylic and silk or rayon blend to allow for maximum drape. Feel free to mix and match any of the charts in this book.

Match the tabby weft to your warp yarn or change tabby weft colors every few inches and insert stripes as you'd like. There are no rules, just have fun with it and create your own magic scarf.

Hand-dyed yarns with subtle variegation work wonderfully.

Weaving Instructions

Warp 62 ends.

With tabby yarn, weave 12 rows. Hemstitch bottom edge.

Choose any chart and complete one full repeat of the stitch pattern. Weave a few rows of tabby, then choose a different chart for the second pattern. Weave another few rows of tabby, then repeat the first stitch pattern.

Continue, alternating plain tabby weave with stitch patterns as desired, changing and mirroring colors within each charted pattern.

With tabby yarn, weave 12 rows. Hemstitch top edge.

Finish, trimming fringe to 3".

Equipment

10" rigid heddle loom or larger with a 7.5 or 8 dent heddle, several
shuttles, pick-up stick,
tapestry needle

Yarn

Warp:
3/2 or 8/4 cotton or cotton blend, size 3 cotton yarn, 60 yds (Valley Yarns, Calley Cotton 3/2, Autumn Blonde)

Weft (tabby):
Sport-weight wool or wool blend, 50 yds (Cloudborn, Superwash Merino Sport Twist, Taupe Heather)

Weft (pattern yarn):
Worsted-weight wool or wool blend, 10 yds each of 6 colors (*Universal Yarn, Deluxe Worsted, Turquoise, Orchid, Lime Tree, Hot Fuscia, Cactus, Blue Lagoon*)

Sett

Warp: 7.5 epi

7.5 epi x 25 ppi = 1" tabby woven on loom

Total warp ends: 62
(60 + 2 for selvedges)

Dimensions

Width on the loom: 7"
Warp length for one mug rug:
34" (10" + 4" for fringe, and 20" for loom waste)
Add 14" to warp for each additional rug

Finished size: 6.5" x 9", without fringe

Weaving Instructions

Warp 62 ends.

With tabby yarn, weave 10 rows. Hemstitch bottom edge.

Work chart from beginning to end, changing color as indicated, cutting and weaving in the pattern yarn tails when they are no longer needed.

With tabby yarn, weave 10 rows. Hemstitch top edge.

Finish and trim fringe to 1.5".

Mix 'n Match Mug Rug

Any of the pattern charts with multiples of 5, 10, and 20 will work with this pattern. Remember to add 2 warps for the selvedges.

I've included graph paper after the projects for you to experiment with. It's a good idea to sketch out different color combinations before you start. Just make copies and grab colored pencils or markers that match your yarn.

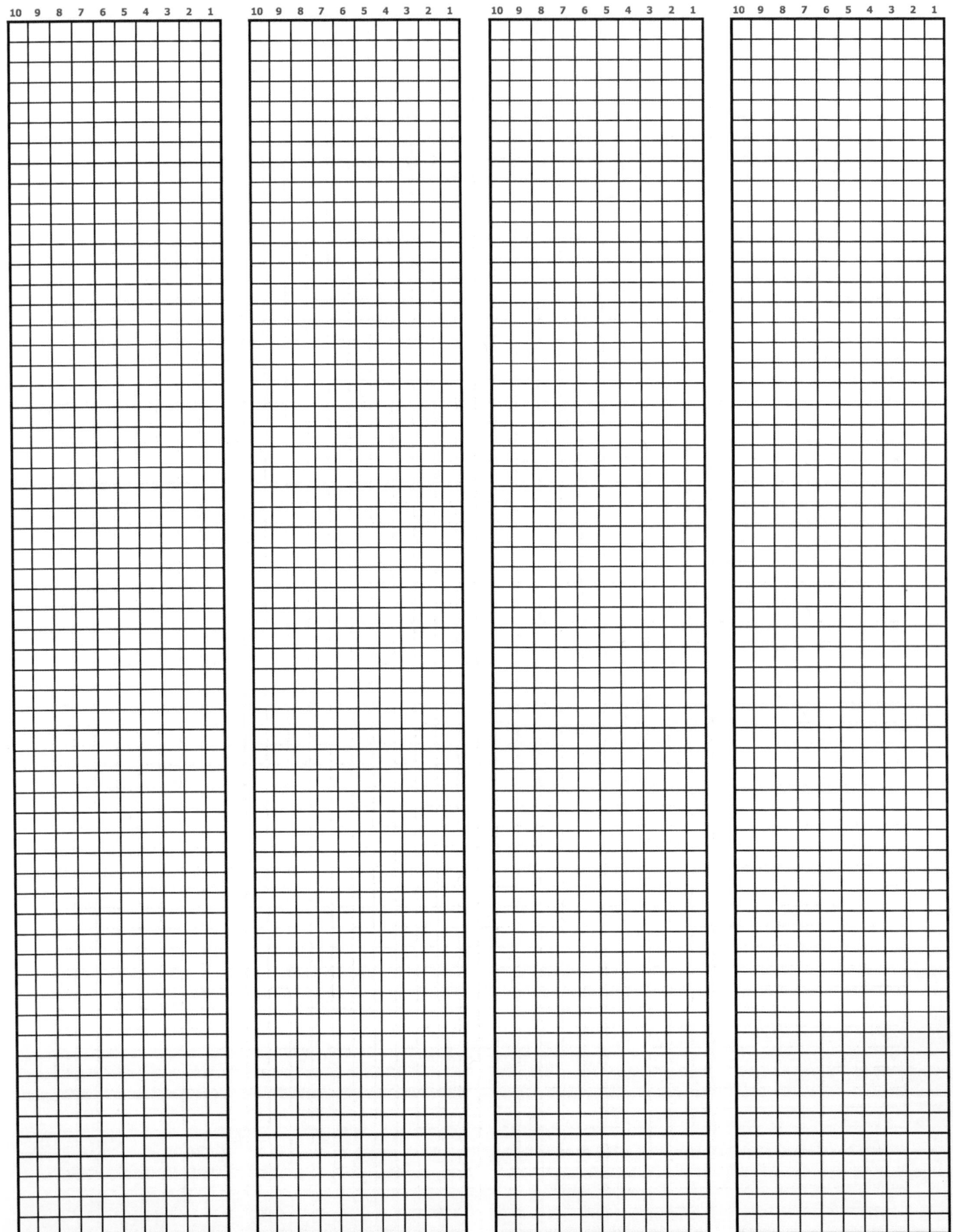

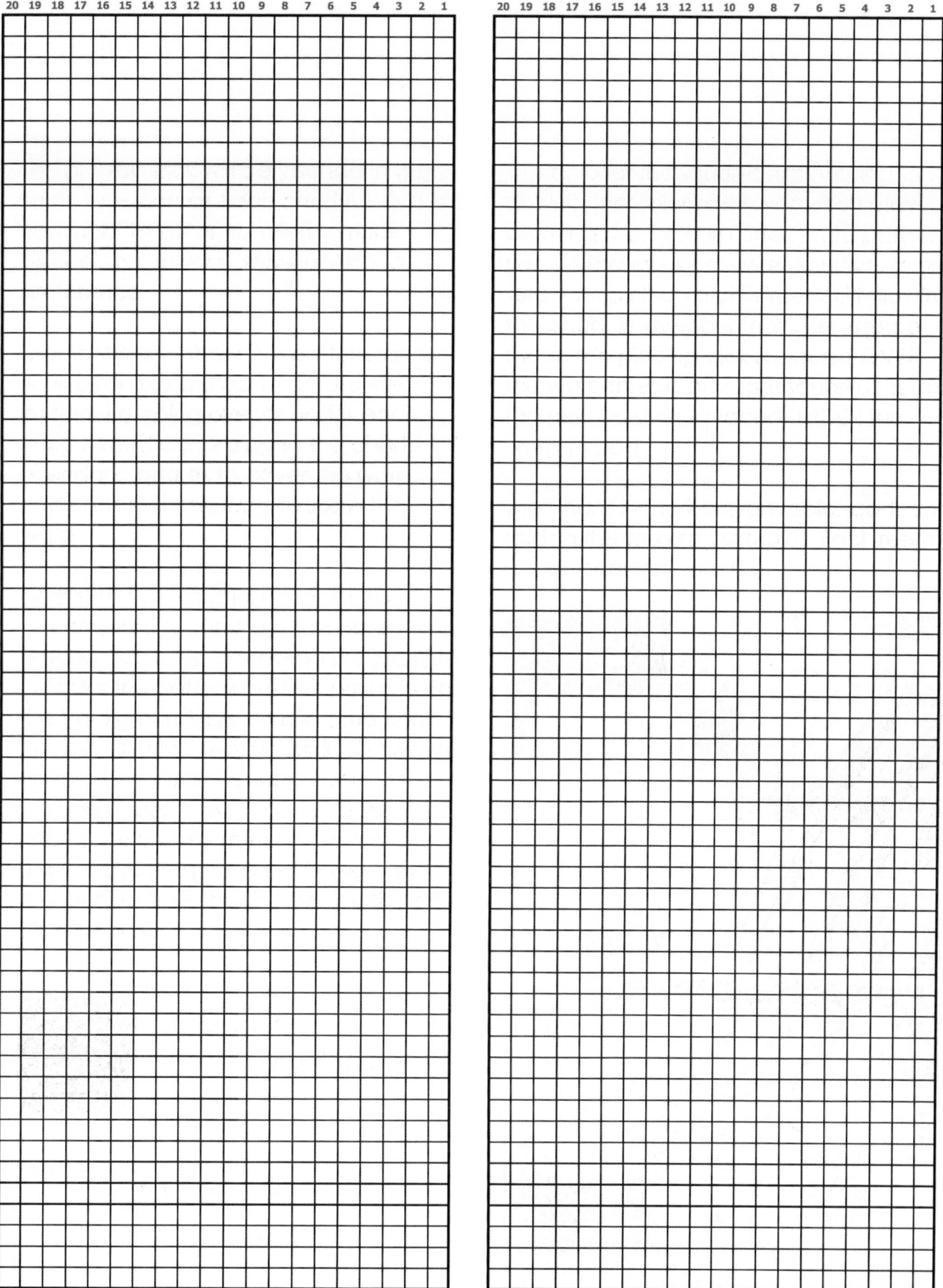

Printed in Great Britain
by Amazon

56085067R00032